Essays on Confidence Games

&

Confidence Men

for the devil in us all

First printing: 2021

Printed in The United States of America

ISBN: 978-1-716-23592-4

Essays on Confidence Games

&

Confidence Men

by

Chris Roy

Previous Publications

Praesidio

Dossier

Praesidio: Revised

Atrophy

Sleight.exe

I Love When You Show Me Magic

The Black Book: Confidence Games

Contents

Foreword

by

Brian Graham

You walk into a cafeteria in a crowded place. There is a wallet, jam packed with cash, just laying on a table, clearly left behind by an unfortunate, forgetful individual. Your first thought is, *could I?* You assess the situation – lots of people, nobody would see you swipe it… or maybe you just pretend it is yours and pick it up with confidence…

Why is the first thought *could I?* and not *should I?* Humans are hard wired to be greedy - to exploit errors. At what point does the fault of taking a forgotten wallet lie on the shoulders of the taker, and not the leaver?

A suggested video pops up in the "recommended" section of your YouTube home page titled *How to Duplicate Money in Video Game X.* You play this game on a daily basis and are not necessarily struggling for in-game money, but you will be damned if you pass up an opportunity to explore something sneaky in the name of excess. Is it your fault for exploiting an in-game bug, or does this fault belong to the game developers?

In the following pages, Chris Roy will thoroughly indulge you with the world of confidence games through realistic hypotheticals, carefully crafted analogies, and unfortunate real-life examples. Give yourself over to Chris Roy, as he sets aside your moral ethics that fight you, tooth and nail, to resist enveloping yourself in the world of exploitation. His essays will guide the mind through the murky waters of *why*, and *what* to do about the urges and sensations caused by confidence games and the feelings of those affected everyday by them.

Introduction

There are many ideas for confidence games and scams that come from exploring old ideas, cutting off the fat and repurposing them to fit into the modern age. This is at the core of most schemes perpetrated nowadays. Perhaps knowing the barebones blueprints for new confidence games can help active self-protectors be cognizant and see the confidence games before they even have to deal with them.

Simply looking at the crimes and the ploys used only paints a partial picture. Psychology is a large area in the world of confidence games, but more specifically the subtleties of how confidence men think and *what* they think about is just as important. As an obsessor of deception, the following pages will be painted with the ideas and thoughts often plaguing my mind and the minds of others in this field.

There are days when the *how* matters much less than the *why*. It is impossible to believe that confidence games are always all about money or valuables. Sometimes, *information* is the sunken treasure or pot of gold at the end of the rainbow.

To better illustrate, and in turn, better help the public understand confidence games, frauds, scams, swindles, street hustles, and schemes the mind must be explored. Criminals and no-good doers are all lumped together in a heap of illegal thinking and acting. But the confidence man is not always a criminal and does not always condone crime. Master manipulators are confidence men at their core, but never took the leap to crime. This is incredibly common.

In video gaming, when a weakness in the software of a game is found that gives an advantage to the player, the player *exploits* this mistake or weakness in the design of the game in order to have an advantage. The developers of the games do not condone

14

these actions and often take great steps to rectify these exploits as they give an unintended advantage to one player over another. Although, any player in theory could discover the exploit, the one who discovers it first reaps the benefits.

Confidence men operate in much the same way, always looking for the exploits in the mistakes and weaknesses in people and in life. When the exploits are no longer viable they are left behind, and new exploits are explored. Life and people are not linear and are always changing. Ideas and lifestyles are being recycled with each new generation. This is why many *old* or *outdated* scams and confidence games continue to make a reappearance, the new generations do not know of them. This is an exploit.

Using simple, but effective confidence games on an unsuspecting person because it was thwarted years ago, but the people who did the thwarting are now dead. Confidence games are rarely the hot topic in the news or media. Murder, robbery, acts of violence, these are the top subjects and confidence games get forgotten. Humanity is doing itself a disservice by not being invested in *all* of the things that could be used to take advantage of them each and every day.

Beyond this introductory chapter will be exploration, observation, and hopefully, understanding by way of short essays and general thoughts.

Deception is a seductive field and confidence games are often shrouded in mysticism and, by way of films and television, even romanticism. They are seen as the push back against regularity and day to day-ness. The ideas and creative brilliance often displayed in these schemes by brilliant and creative people are shunned simply because they are, by virtue, manipulative and deceptive. If appreciation can be shown, understanding can be had. Every time a new serial killer documentary is released on your favorite streaming service the masses huddle around their televisions, laptops, tablets, and smart phones like it is the last flame of humanity. Our brains are pumped full of stories about brutal crimes we would otherwise never see or want to see. This obsession seems to be perfectly acceptable by society. This is an obsession with the worst humanity has to offer but because it is so largely accepted no one can call it for what it is, obsession with deception.

Much of what will be read in these pages are opinions and mindless musings about confidence games and confidence men with the purpose that my previous publications had, challenge ideas but also encourage people to *think*. Blindly accepting what people say and do around us is how we get caught in scams and confidence games to begin with. These essays should do no more than help the reader think about confidence games in a manner that can become habitual.

Not all ideas found here will be strong opinions or even strong ideas. They serve their purpose though. Some ideas are downright silly, but others are a bit more serious.

Some included essays are from previous publications by this author as to compile them in a single anthology and to bring more attention to them. These ideas, concepts, and opinions can be lost in the sea of chapters of other books, scattered across several titles. Where essays have been added as not original to this publication an indication may be made.

Doing Good Things

"Just because a person starts doing good things does not mean they want to stop doing bad things."[1]

There has to be some understanding that when a person starts doing something it does not mean they have stopped doing the opposite. Of course, this only applies when both avenues can be taken. The opposite of being alive is being dead, and short of laying in Schrödinger's[2] coffin it probably should be left to wild theorists. If a person drives a motorcycle and begins driving a car, it does not inherently mean they have given up on the motorcycle.

---

[1] Quote taken from the television series *White Collar*. Season 5, episode 4: *Controlling Interest*

[2] A reference to a thought experiment whereby a cat in a box must be presumed alive and dead at the same time. A paradox for this hypothetical feline.

It is this area of thought that lends itself to thinking about wanting to do good deeds, even though bad deeds have been laid out in the past. As a person starts doing good things, it is possible it can outweigh the *bad* they have done. It is far more likely that a life of good can be undone by wrong doing than a life of bad can be undone by good deeds. We all want our fellow man to do good, as we do not want to be victimized. This is human nature. Yet, we lord over the heads of people doing bad things and cannot fathom a good deed having much meaning. When this is the case there is now no incentive for a positive change in character and actions.

Living a coexistence of wanting to do good but not wanting to give up the bad is a struggle. *Bad* does not have to mean evil but could mean not exactly upstanding. Something along the lines of seeing someone drop five dollars on the ground and not telling them and keeping it. Is this person evil simply because they did not feel the obligation to inform this person? If it was a cell phone would the circumstances change? Every person uses deceit and deception in their life. Most people use it daily! *No one is perfect.* This has never meant to me that people make mistakes but instead that people are not always *good*, they certainly do not always choose the most morally right choices. This must mean there is some level of *bad* that we all tolerate. Some levels are higher and tolerated due to circumstances and situation. Is killing wrong? Sure. Is killing someone who is attempting to kill thousands of people okay? Well, eh. Who knows? That is the point! No one knows for sure. This is a bit grandiose as an example, but the reader was promised illustration through words.

Determining at what level a person can be redeemed or not redeemed will be an argument had until the world collapses and we all return to dust.

This is no advocacy for bad things as long as people do good things to balance it.

It is a call to understanding that bad people can do good things and good people can do bad things.

Longer You Go

Often, the question is raised, *when does one stop, when does one get out of the game?* Truth is, most people never do. Once a confidence man, always a confidence man. They may not commit crimes or exploit those around them, but they always see the angles. Getting *out of the game* realistically refers to someone no longer committing crimes. Whether they are caught or not.

There can be a whole slew of reasons for someone wanting to get out, tired of living on the run, falling ill, or even falling in love. The confidence man could find themselves with a family and does not want to put them in harm's way, and they give up the chase.

"The longer you go, the less the money matters. The food doesn't taste as good. The cars aren't fast enough. The view isn't high enough. And finally, you realize that you would trade it

all in for one night of going to bed, where you don't have to worry, 'When are they going to come for me?'[3]

In years, never has there been such a quote that could sum up the idea of getting out of the life. It can all be summed up even further in saying, *it is not worth it anymore.* This is a reason above most, afraid of losing freedom. Which is what being a confidence man is all about. Having freedom and doing what is wanted and having what is wanted. Freedom to go anywhere and be anyone. The idea of losing this intoxication of freedom can be all it takes. It certainly was a factor for me.

Whatever reason a person has for giving up this lifestyle, it is for the best. Take what is learned, lessons embodied, and skills acquired to help others or put those areas of knowledge into a new, less harmful, craft.

---

[3] Quote taken from the television series *Suits.* Season 5, episode 9: *Uninvited Guests*

Exploits

As mentioned in the introduction, there are exploits all around us. Loopholes to be manipulated and, well, *exploited*. Circumventing programs, people, and rules are always going to be a part of life. Should all the people who take full advantage of these instances be held liable, even though anyone could use the exploit? Is it up to the public to inform a company or business that they have a crack in their system?

It can be difficult to have any sympathy for a multi-million dollar company who did not hire someone smart enough to close a loophole in a contract that gives the consumer a tremendous deal the company never intended the consumer to have. Taking the exploit to a higher level is where confidence men operate, and they are often looked down upon or charged with criminal offences for these actions. Without people in positions to look for exploits and loopholes they would never be patched up.

Extreme couponing[4] is a form of exploiting a system in groceries stores and retailers. Often, these extreme *couponers*[5] receive money back or pay nearly nothing for their hundreds of dollars' worth of goods. They are doing what any other person could do but has not put the effort into in order to accomplish. Should this be frowned upon? They are not paying for their groceries. Is this not a bad thing? They used what was made available by the retailer in a way that was advantageous.

Ask any moderately serious gamer, they will likely say exploits are fair use as long as everyone has equal access to them. Nothing the player is doing makes the

---

[4] Couponing is a verb used to describe collecting coupons from retailers and grocers and using them to obtain discounts when purchasing in stores or online.
[5] A couponer is someone who practices couponing. Extreme couponing is at a level well beyond that of a normal shopper or couponer.

exploit more attainable to them than another player. The only party being exploited is the game itself, not other players. *Unless the exploit is in a multiplayer version of the game.* This is not the same as cheating or hacking or *modding*[6] as no outside adjustments are made by the player. They are not introducing something to the game that was not already there.

If a vending machine has a button that always gives a free drink when pressed, even though it was an accidental design flaw, is the person pressing the button a bad person for using it? If that same person had used a tool to reach behind the button and make it give free drinks that would be an external force being introduced and changing the outcome of the situation.

Examples of real life exploits can be found everywhere. The argument of *are*

---

[6] The act of changing the behavior or appearance of a game to something other than intended by the developers.

exploits OK? is a side argument to *exploiting individuals is bad and exploiting large companies is fine?* Using an exploit to help oneself can be seen as a grey area, but using them when they hurt others, regardless of if they help someone, seems to negate their argument for purpose.

It is impossible to draw an accurate line as to where exploits are perfectly acceptable and where they are not. The argument against lies and deception gets hashed every day. *When is it acceptable to lie or to deceive someone?* The same goes for exploits, when are they acceptable?

Some would argue lies and deception are never acceptable. Others would argue that under certain or specific circumstances they can be useful and often beneficial for greater good. Police officers are well within the scope of their job to lie to suspects of crimes. This is how undercover police officers and federal agents can be effective. There is a myth that police officers are required to inform someone if they are a police officer if asked, this is untrue and speaks to the point that deception helps law enforcement. If a suspected criminal asks an undercover officer if they are an officer, believing the officer cannot lie, the officer can say *no* and thus the suspected criminal will be working without that information and the government can build a case against them. In this example the officer *exploited* a known fallacy in the understanding of operations of law enforcement by the public.

Caliber

Lumping all forms of deception specialists into one group is a disservice and a step in the wrong direction of understanding the exploits around us. The caliber at which deceptive practitioners operate says a lot about them and their exploits.

To better illustrate this point, if there is a gym full of basketball players does this mean automatically that all of the players are at the same skill level? Or that they compete at the same level? No, it does not. There is an inherit understanding that a professional athlete is at a higher level of performance than that of a college athlete or weekend hobbyist, typically. The same applies to criminals and more specifically, confidence men, scammers, grifters, swindlers.

The hierarchy is still to be determined, but here is what it could possibly look like in order from top to bottom: Confidence men, grifters, swindlers, scammers. These terms are not always interchangeable. Scammers use a blanket to cast over large groups in order to get a hit and focus in on the kill. Confidence men exploit opportunities and zero in on specific individuals right from the outset.

Why does this matter?

If one is to understand these individuals, one has to understand that calling everyone a scammer who commits fraud, or hustles at billiards, or sells counterfeit art sets up the public to misunderstand the threats against them. Scammers are a dime a dozen and can be thwarted with much less effort than that of a professional confidence man or career grifter.

There is no single piece of advice or method for stopping neither scams nor confidence games. When broken into separate categories they need their own prescription to be combatted. And further, each individual scam or confidence game has to be treated directly if it is to be prevented, stopped, or figured out.

If confidence men are leading the field they should be the biggest problem addressed, right? Not necessarily. Scammers have the habit of reaching many more people, this creates more possible victims. Scammers are a dime a dozen, and anyone could sling a pot of digital cream corn and hit a scammer on any number of social media sites, forums, and other platforms.

Is Everything a Scam?

There is not much that needs to be said in this essay, because the fact is that not every bad deal or terrible price for a product or service is a scam. A bad deal is not a scam. If a business or person offers a service or product at a publicly advertised price and changes the price to a higher one once customers come for the products or services that would be a scam. If a business or person is offering a product at 10x the current market value, that is not a scam, that is simply not a good price and soon enough that business or person will not be able to compete in the market because their prices are unreasonable.

By calling all objectively bad deals *scams* it lowers the threshold and standard of what a scam is, and the public cannot differentiate between legitimate scams and bad deals. If everything is a scam, nothing is a scam. There are those who would say that casinos are scams. Or that the lottery is a scam. Casinos are like any other business. They peddle entertainment and the not-so elusive chance to garner a payday with the right play and a bit of luck. There are no guarantees going into a casino and playing any of their games. Just as there is no guarantee of winning the lottery if played.

> *"Some of us are too timid to risk a dollar, but the percentage of people in this feverish nation who would not enjoy winning one is very small."*[7]

No one is forced to go to casinos or play the lottery, they are ecstatic if they win and furious if they lose. The logic behind downplaying ideas and subjects that we do not understand or that have not given us an incredible boost in some way is flawed.

If a person cannot take full advantage of opportunities or chances placed at their feet it does not make the opportunities or

---

[7] Quoted from the preface of *The Expert at the Card Table* by S. W. Erdnase. 1902.

chances poor. Sometimes people do not make great decisions. This could be from a lack of understanding, logic, reasoning, knowledge or deductive abilities. Thus, they claim these opportunities to be scams and tell others to avoid them.

This obscure blanket is cast over the life course of going to college or university as well. It can cost large sums of money to attend courses and if one person does not acquire the same outcome as another student or the outcome they would have liked they exclaim how college is a big fat stinky scam. They could not get the dream job after college? Scam. It just did not work out. By passing blame on *scams* out there in the ether it will be impossible to make the appropriate changes to systems, markets, and structures so everyone can prosper. And *if* college were a scam it would go to the point outlined in previous publications that anyone can be a victim, and no one is too smart to be scammed or conned.

Personal Responsibility

As a society, criminals and wrongdoers are held accountable for imposing their intentions and crimes on other citizens. Through criminal and civil legal proceedings, criminals can be forced to acknowledge their responsibilities as a citizen. *Should citizens be held personally responsible for their actions that allow opportunities to sprout for greedy individuals?* If someone leaves their wallet on a table and walks away for an extended period, at what point does the personal responsibility shift onto the person who comes along and steals the wallet?

This essay is in no way condoning theft, or crime of any sort. Nor is this essay blaming victims of crimes for being victims. There might be a personal responsibility to protect oneself and one's belongings by being informed and educated on the criminal activities and proclivities of morally sub-par characters. There is no excuse for anyone who commits crimes, this essay does not wish to create one. Individual situations could very often be avoided by simply being prepared to avoid them. Instead of hoping that people do not commit crimes, there is a police force and a legal system. The utopian idea of *people should just always do the right thing* is, sadly, not the reality of the existence we all share in some way or another. A disservice is being done if responsible people act in an irresponsible manner with their own safety.

If raw poultry is left unattended on a kitchen counter for an extended period of time it will begin to develop bacteria for *E. coli*, if ingested can make even the most iron-stomached individual beg for mercy. Instead of blaming the *E. coli* for developing, precautions are taken against it. Now, people have freewill and choice and this analogy is not supposed to be the end of the conversation. It simply demonstrates a point that sometimes precautions are necessary.

What can be done to prevent being scammed? Or to thwart a confidence man from taking your company for millions? Is it even possible to stop these people from achieving their goals of exploitation?

The preventative measures against scams, frauds, confidence games, swindles, and street hustles all begin with acceptance and awareness, being able to accept that there are individuals who are looking to take advantage of others and being aware that paths may cross with these individuals any time. Understand that there is no *free, no strings attached* money floating around waiting for someone to come along and claim it. *Too good to be true* is the perfect phrase to begin the path to awareness and protection from confidence games.

Ask questions, be inquisitive when conducting business with anyone. If business is initiated by the other party guards should be up to prevent falling into something too quickly.

Misinforming the Masses

The part time job and hobby of all deception practitioners is that of keeping the general populous oblivious to their operations and the mechanics of said operations. The greatest example of misinformation being spread is through the street hustle, *three card monte.* A true classic in the world of confidence games. It has all of the levels and layers, all of the characters and players, all of the dynamics needed for the perfect model of a confidence game.

In three card monte, players are led to believe if they can win money by attempting to correctly guess the position of one card among three cards all placed face down. This *game* is unwinnable. Through the use of sleight of hand and, what seems like, made up rules (because they are made up). The public who have heard of this short confidence game often believe that they would be allowed to win one or even two smaller bets to get *buttered up,* and this is not true in the slightest. There is almost no circumstance where players will be allowed to win some sort of sympathy bet or greasing bet.

This piece of misinformation causes *more* players to play this *game* under the guise that they can win a small bet and walk away. It creates more marks and victims. Three card monte perfectly demonstrates how misinformation perpetuated by confidence men, scammers, or even those who have the intention to prevent scams can create more victims and lead to ongoing confidence games. There is no reason for three card monte hustlers to stop if the public thinks they are letting people win small amounts of money. Once a bet is placed they have already hooked the mark. There is no reason to allow any money to part the hustlers pocket. Often, others in the field of deception who wish to do good and *help* the masses actually do harm by speaking on this subject specifically, stating that monte hustlers allow *players* to win a small bet in order to hook them or rope them into a game. If the mark is betting at all they are already roped into the game.

It is dangerous to ever believe there is an instance where a mark could come out ahead in any circumstance involving confidence games. This level of perpetuated misinformation is precisely what confidence men need in order to *stay in business.*

In order to keep the clueless masses oblivious to confidence games and their mechanics, misinformation is spread to allow for much more difficult attempts at identifying confidence games and thwarting them. If we choose not to accept that confidence men already have a leg up on us we will be woefully unprepared to engage them in any meaningful manner. Whether that is affecting change or seeking to punish them.

When material is published, articles are written, and videos are shot, in many cases an actual confidence man is not consulted for that project or piece of publication or literature. This may be difficult to do as most confidence men would certainly like to remain anonymous. So-called *experts* are sometimes brought in to answer some general questions and give a general sense of confidence games and confidence men. When this is done there are some instances where terms are interchanged and used inaccurately and inappropriately, because *who is going to correct them?* Is a confidence man going to come forth and make the necessary corrections and fact checks required?

Contrast

This chapter was originally going to be titled *Scammers Versus Confidence Men*. However, the word *versus* really lends itself to a different type of discussion than is appropriate here. There are many similarities between these two groupings and a lot of overlap. The desire here is not to pit one group against the other or in any way imply that one is *better* than the other.

Why would such a statement even matter? Both are criminals, right? Both take advantage of other people, correct? The answer is, *eh*. A true confidence man or con artist uses finesse and an array of talents and skills to get over on a mark. The typical mark of a true conman is someone (or some business) that has it to lose. If asked, a real conman might say that they stay away from three types of people; the elderly, children, and anyone disabled or handicapped. This includes businesses that have these groups of people as their primary clients and customers. It is not a guarantee and conmen sometimes do go after these people. There is no perfect equation for dictating marks.

Misconceptions are an inescapable reality faced each day in this world. Information is gathered improperly, stored, and then shared incorrectly. In many cases, this bit of information becomes a factoid and does not harm the overall course of life or in any way really influence society at all. There are instances that do cause more harm than good though. Under the umbrella of deceptions relating to the work of confidence men and scammers, this can seem like it is a valuable tool and it is for those respective categories of people, but the general public is misinformed as to what these people do, how they do it, and their motivations.

When it comes to misconceptions it is easy to blame the people who are misinformed. This is unfair if that group of people was given information from a source they trust or a reliable informant like a news outlet for instance. There has been a serious trend in the news, and related sources, of scams being labeled under cons (confidence games). This form of misinformation leads people to think they know enough to avoid being conned under the guise that they are avoiding being scammed. There is overlap in these two areas of deception, but they are in no way identified as the same.

Scammers

Using aggression, speed, and pure lies the scammer aims to achieve their goals. Whether one victim figures out their plan or not, they will move from victim to victim with very minimal time being spent to acquire what they are after. This could include money, personal information, or valuable goods (e.g. cell phones, laptops). Using the overwhelming number of victims, the scammers do not have to be especially charismatic or likable. If their ploy fails, they could get more aggressive and even violent to get what they want. There is a fine line between common thieves, scammers, and confidence men. The scammer operates close to both lines until one fails. The moral latitude of what I would describe as scammers is much lower in my experience than that of con men. Scammers will go after almost anyone in the victim pool, including elderly, disabled, and any others they can exploit. They keep their contact minimal until they either get what they want, or the scam falls apart (and it often does). Scammers target weaker individuals and do not typically engage with people they consider to be too much trouble. Scammers rely heavily on their anonymity, especially if using the internet for their scamming purposes.

Scammers rely heavily on anonymity in order to complete their blanket objectives. They hide in the ocean of the internet and the sea of people around the world. Being just another face is part of their character design. Below average speaking ability in target language, delays and randomness in communication, quick frustration with mark or victim, forceful propositions and requests, time constraints, and generic language are all signs someone could be in communication with a scammer. Whether in person or on the internet.

Confidence men

A different breed of *criminal* from any other on Earth, the confidence man has a level of finesse and grace that scammers just do not possess. They have honed a vast number of skills, they are adept at research, and talking their way into riches is what they pride themselves on. They are liars as well and they do have a low moral standard, but it is still much higher than that of a scammer. They will get face to face and do what they have to do and leave a lot of people out of it. Now, not all confidence men are the high stepping, $5000 suit-wearing gentlemen that is seen often on television and in movies. The con man, or *con artist*, as they are sometimes referred, have refined their crimes to a small victim pool and the payoff is generally much higher than that of a petty scam. Scammers use quantity to make their money and con men focus in on a specific mark and take their time earning their dollars and cents.

Unlike their deceptive counterparts, scammers, confidence men do not always rely on anonymity to accomplish their goals. Face-to-face interactions are how confidence men instill trusts and build confidence from marks. They need their would-be victims to see them and trust them.

Fine Line

The purpose for entries such as this one is to properly educate the public on what it is to be a scammer and what it is to be a confidence man. A scammer is a simpler version and whenever there is a *clever* crime the authorities or the news would like to lump everyone together and this serves a reverse purpose and actually gives the confidence men a place to hide and more importantly a place to cover their previous more high-profile crimes. Scams are much easier to spot than a confidence game is to spot. People begin to believe that since they are not seeing anything and are not catching scammers then they must not be victims of anything. This just lulls them to sleep for the con artist to craft a perfectly laid plan that they will hatch at the most unforeseen moment. Do not let yourself fall to the idea that you are too smart or that there is a *Top 5 Ways to Spot Scams*. Both of these things are not true, and one would only be more open to both scams and confidence games.

If someone wishes to protect themselves, ask questions, be vigilant. The sooner they accept there are things they do not know, they will already have more power than they did before.

The everyday person does not always need to make these distinctions between scammers and confidence men. This is to bring awareness to a field that is misunderstood, misdiagnosed, and improperly handled regularly.

False Confidence

In some instances, when a scam is perpetrated it will not go well for the scammer. This could be because they are inexperienced, the situation has too many variables, or there was an outside influence that changed the scenario. Whatever the reason, if it does not go well for the scammer and they are thwarted, the person who does the thwarting often times becomes overconfident that they are equipped to stop scammers or that they are no longer able to be scammed.

A person could know every scam and confidence game in the world and still never be perfectly safe from them.

I have seen and read many accounts of people tripping up a scammer during his ruse and then they begin to try and inform others as to how to stop them. For the most part, when someone does not get scammed or conned, it is because they were just lucky, or the so-called scammer was so new that he could barely be called that.

A sense of confidence is now mistakenly instilled in this person. Just because they may have inadvertently stopped a scam from unfolding in front of them does not mean that someone else will not fall for it. There are a lot of variations and variables to every deception and they are often times tailored as best they can be for specific situations.

After these stories, they are often followed by, *who would fall for that?* Your mother, brother, cousin, friend, roommate, doctor, lawyer. That is who would fall for it. There is no one type of person that is immune.

Intelligence leads to hubris which leads to a much lighter wallet. Damages can be lessened, and problems can be mitigated by being well informed and by thinking things out before action is taken.

Jane

Every day is a chance to find some inspiration. As a writer, every book read, every show watched, and every person talked to could possibly lead to an idea for a new piece to be written. Sometimes these ideas come organically and other times they come after more reflection. When deciding what to write I ask myself if the piece should be more entertaining or if it should focus solely on educating the reader. Even after I make that decision it usually turns to shit because it does not feel like a natural way to write.

I have come across a few articles and a few videos (some sent directly to me) that have to do with civilians trying to sign up for scams and then film it and see where it leads. That is the gist of what has been gathered from these videos and articles. The reporter, or journalist, or grad student decides to email back the sender of an *All Expense Vacation*

Paid Winner email or call back the fake IRS call and basically, *see what happens*, as they put it.

Before I break down my thoughts on this particular subject I want to say, I am always in agreement that you should do your research and be well informed. This is especially true in areas that could cause you harm or problems in the future. There is no knowledge that is not power.

In the scenario I would like to discuss, we have a nice female reporter (who will be referred to as *Jane*[8]) who goes undercover to an entity claiming to give away free cruises to everyone who received an email. This is a very regular and not very creative ploy, but it gets the job done for these scammers. Jane goes to an address that she was given that says she just has to sit in for a business pitch and then she will receive the free cruise! Easy enough, right? Hell yes.

---

[8] Her real name has been kept out of this book to save her any embarrassment and to protect her privacy.

But as time goes on there are more hoops and this dog is tired of jumping. Jane grabs her cameraman and they storm the room and start demanding answers to questions like *Where is my free cruise, is this a scam, why are you scamming people?*

It goes on like this and the gentleman running this ring of perpetual free cruises finally sends her away after deciding not to answer any more questions. To be fair, Jane sat through all the offers and talks and did so quietly and politely. However, after the sessions end she does something I do not recommend to *any person, ever.* She confronted the person she believes is scamming her, *in person.*

There are many things wrong with this scenario. First, even if she goes through the motions knowing it is a scam, that does not save her! Just because she believes that the scammers want a particular piece of information from her, they may actually want a completely different piece of information that she gave because she did not find it relevant and thought it was harmless at the time. She could end up hurting herself and falling for the real scam while thinking it is a scam for something else.

For instance, you come to the scammer's business front and they have valet only parking. You give your keys to the valet and go inside ready to bust some no-good crooks. Well, guess what, idiot? You just gave the valet driver access to your registration which typically has your address on it and oh yeah, your house keys!

While you are in the scammer's little presentation, they have made a copy of your keys and got your address. Now you are more likely to be robbed than to fall for the scam you were there for. Hell, you might become a victim of both! I do not blame the victims of scams because it could truly happen to anyone but when you seek out these types of people then you are deserving of anything that happens to you.

Let us say she is lucky to get a few generalized answers to her highly inflammatory questions; how does she think the scammers are going to handle this type of situation? She could be putting them in a lot of trouble. They are not likely to look kindly on this and she could be in danger physically at this point. She could be kidnapped, beaten, or even killed (and yes, this has happened and does happen). These criminals are not going to let some pumped up reporter or student get in the way of their money and ruin what they have going on.

I have been in the lion's den of many scams and criminal enterprises in order to do research, but I approached it in a much less accusatory way. I knew what I was doing, and I fully understood where it could leave me. Doing these things in order to catch someone in the act and shame them is not a good strategy at all. This goes for all the *caught in the act* videos that can be seen on the internet.

Avoid these scams and scammers, and do not think you are smarter than them. Thinking you are smarter is exactly what *professionals* want. They want you to give yourself a false sense of security by thinking you can outwit them. Mostly it happens by shear chance and luck. It is not your business or your place to crack the case and expose these people. I know you think you are doing the right thing, but you are doing it the wrong way.

Truth be told, vigilantism probably has a place in society for these types of situations. However, doing it in a reckless manner does no one any good. Most people would agree that scammers should get what is coming to them, but in the way that does not put more people in harm's way to do it.

Grifter

Perhaps the pinochle of what it is to be a professional or lifelong deceiver is the *grifter*. Someone whose sole existence is committed to not being committed. They say what they need to say, do what they need to do, and be who they need to be in order to maintain their own lifestyle and assert their will on the world and anyone they cross paths with.

Grifters are not as actively malicious as a scammer, whose sole purpose is to take advantage of as many people for as much as possible, but to put as many variables in their favor as possible by misleading people, lying, and taking on personas that best fit their needs.

Benefits to a grifter do not always mean money or valuables. A benefit could be information or access to a place they could not access before, like backstage at a concert.

Now, some of these examples are a bit silly and should not be considered a grifter's first choice of deception, but they make the point.

Grifters do want money and they can be classified as confidence men sometimes. The two are almost interchangeable. A conman could be running one long con and still be considered a conman. A grifter has made a life of living this way. A conman could too, and he would be a grifter in that scenario as well.

Sometimes the drive is pure sport, sometimes it could be a thrill, other times it is out of a necessity that grifters attempt to swindle, con, or manipulate those around them. There is not a single equation to fill in the blanks and tell anyone what a grifter's goals and desires are. They change with each grifter.

Some are marked with the travel bug, meaning they are not stationary and set in one city. They may not call any place home at all. Living life on the road allows them to stay void of close relationships. Although, they will be quite adept at quickly forming personal bonds with individuals they meet on their journey.

Myths

Working in an industry revolving around sharing information about confidence games, frauds, and white collar crime often there are questions asked or statements made that spark a new conversation and explanation for listeners and readers. Based on these questions and statements a list has been compiled to debunk myths about these topics. In no particular order. This list should not be considered complete or comprehensive.

Only dumb people fall for scams.

While being intelligent or smarter than the people around you can be a tremendous advantage, when it comes to confidence games and scams that is not a safety net. Sure, a person may see through a ruse poorly executed, but every person on Earth is susceptible to be taken advantage of. Being vigilant is just as important as being intelligent and perhaps more so. Being wary of a dream come true is the first step.

Scams involve large sums of money.

Many scams that exist are to relieve a person of their immediate cash or belongings. Three Card Monte on a dirty street corner can only take what money is readily available to the scamming dealer and his crew. These types of scammers do not take checks. There may be phishing scams or romance scams that last longer and slowly get a victim or mark to trickle the money out of the wallet and accounts. Large sums of money being given up should always be looked at with due diligence.

You are smarter than scammers and confidence men.

You are not. This one might sting a little but allow an explanation. You may be able to thwart a failed attempt by a pick pocket or a cold call from a boiler room attempting their best *Wolf of Wall Street*[9] impression, but that is a temporary lapse and you are an anomaly in that instance. There is a reason that law enforcement's main objective is to catch criminals and not stop them. Because everyone is playing from behind. If so many people were smarter than scammers, we would not have nearly as many. Thinking yourself too smart only leads to letting your guard down. Keep a watchful eye and that will be your best weapon. Do not try to outthink a scammer. Avoid them if at all possible. There is a specific confidence game design for this very situation, *Kansas City Shuffle*[10]. All of this is not to say they are smarter than you, but when it comes to being a criminal they

---

[9] The *Wolf of Wall Street* is a memoir by Jordan Belfort, 2007. It is also a film starring Leonardo DiCaprio as Belfort in 2013. It is about corrupt and greedy stock brokers.

[10] A confidence game whereby the mark is intentionally led to believe that they have figured out the confidence game, but this is actually what the confidence man wants.

probably have the upper-hand. This is their life, you are just a tourist in their world of deception. Be on guard.

Scams are not that rampant.

The Better Business Bureau reports[11] that one in five people are victims of scams and frauds every single year. Amongst a group of five friends, within five years they all could have been scammed. Now this is an extreme example, as there are many factors that go into these types of statistics. The numbers are likely much higher as victims are often embarrassed or unaware they have been taken advantage of to report it. Information is your tool. Just knowing they are out there will help you keep your eyes open.

---

[11] Better Business Bureau infographic, *5 Myths About Scams. #3. 2016.*

Differences

In a previous chapter[12], there were some comparisons and contrasts made between *confidence men* and *scammers* and now we must discuss some other groups and labels that need a spotlight of comparison and contrast but do not warrant as much page space.

As was discussed, confidence men and scammers are not the same. But along with those are *grifters* and *liars.*

All four of these labels are not interchangeable. Often in media and news outlets these terms get randomly pulled from a hat to fit the article or news story better. Conmen, scammers, and grifters all tell lies, but not all liars are conmen, scammers, or grifters. In fact, it could be said that only a small portion of them are. The difference

---

[12] Page 47, Contrast.

here being that the first three are calculating and skillful, whereas a liar is just a liar. They tell lies that may temporarily help them but with no consequence for the future or how it could actually harm them in the short run and long run.

A scammer is a blanket attacker when it comes to deceit. They will reach as many people as possible and shotgun their scam onto anyone and everyone they can. But they have a plan and often a script to take it to the end zone.

A confidence man seeks to hone in on individuals and exploit the greed they may be harboring or their trustworthiness. Emphasizing a specific situation for personal gain is their operation.

Grifters certainly lie and deceive but not always for some dramatic reason. Telling lies is not always the answer to their problems. Recognizing this is what separates them from liars. Liars lie because they can and for no other reason than to do it in many cases.

Confidence men do not *scam*, they *con*. Hints the name. Scammers scam. Grifter grift. Liars lie. A confidence man can perpetrate a scam, but a scammer cannot con, else they would become a conman by virtue.

Why is any of this important? We cannot begin to help victims if we cannot even understand what we are all up against. A hall monitor and a police officer have similar jobs at their core, but the more explanation each one gets, the more we see they are vastly different. A police officer and an agent of the F.B.I. are very similar but very different. They operate at different levels. That is where we see the difference in the individuals described above. They are similar but operate at different levels and in different ways. If we are only looking for the symptoms of scammers we might miss the other individuals right in front of us.

Often when reading an article about confidence games or scams one can tell that it was written with almost no preparation or by someone with no inside knowledge based solely on the terms listed here being interchanged almost randomly and at will.

Magicians

Where do *magicians* fit into this discussion on deception? The truth is, they do not really fit in anywhere. As what they are striving to perfect is for entertainment purposes. Magicians tell you they are going to lie, and they do. They tell you they are going to misdirect, and they do. They tell you they are going to do things right under your nose, and they do. Try to bust them and you will not be able to do it.

I, myself, am a magician and have been for many years. There are times where I might have wanted to mislead a spectator in a very direct manor and say something very untrue to make them look bad or to make the effect I was performing go off even better. The reason I always resisted this urge was that there is not supposed to be any malice in this art form. Using lies and deceit to take advantage of someone and harm them is what separates an entertainer from someone with more pliable morals.

The line between what is right and wrong comes down to the intention of the actions and the preparation beforehand to protect anyone coming into contact with the deception.

"The intricacies of deception can only be fully appreciated through exposure. The magician will protect the laymen from this art so that he can showcase it as something that it is not. The player will protect his art from everybody, for in his eyes, we are all his potential opponents. Deception is a beautiful art often devastated by the hands of magicians. The artist and magician are separated by their perception of the exposure of deception."[13]

---

[13] Quote is from *Exposure*, a video on YouTube and a book produced and published by Daniel Madison.

Should We?

Should we put spotlights on how crimes are committed? Should we draw attention to the deceptions all around us and expose their methods?

There is one thing that should be sought after in learning about confidence games, understanding. If we can understand confidence games, there is a greater chance of avoiding them and more room to help those who have been victimized.

There is a great dilemma for anyone in a profession that seeks to expose crimes of any kind, will this create more criminals? There is no way to know for sure. In efforts to expose methods there is always a chance that too much information will be shared and someone with proclivities to doing bad things might use the information to do harm. This is a necessary risk. We can limit our information on certain subjects because they are truly so simple yet so damaging that we do not want anyone out there to even attempt to follow those blue prints.

There are areas of deception that might be difficult to execute, like a lapping scheme, a form of embezzlement. Or Three Card Monte, a classic street hustle that takes sleight of hand ability, coordination, money, and finesse. The moves could be taught here, and they have been taught in many places but that does not breed more monte dealers because it takes more than swift hands to pull it off.

The more you know about something the less you will be afraid of it and the less power it has over you. We want to give you control with our information and our articles. Whether you read this book or hear a live lecture you will be guided with information, you get to be the one who gets to make the decisions. You get to be the one who decides what happens when you interact with someone you suspect might be out to take advantage of you. There is no knowledge that is not power.

One Question

There is possibly no question asked in regard to scams, frauds, or confidence games more than:

Who would fall for that?

This question, although only a question, infers that the person asking would not have fallen for whatever ploy was being discussed previously. This is a misguided and arrogant way of thinking. It is dangerous and breeds invitations to be scammed.

We all want to believe ourselves to be intelligent and sharp. *No blasted man on the street with three cards is going to swindle me.* They may be correct. But that is only a drop of a drop in a bucket of confidence games that can be introduced to a person to get them on tilt and crack their wallet.

By believing you cannot be taken advantage of only closes doors in ways of thinking. You stop looking for the signs and you do not see them until it is too late. There is a scam, or fraud, or confidence game, or street hustle for every person on Earth. No one is immune. Being poor does not even make you immune, as you could be set up as a patsy and take the fall for someone else. All because you wanted to help a friend. This is not to say you should not help friends, but to say that no one is impermeable.

Someone implying they are immune to scams or confidence games is like saying they are immune to crime. Does not make sense, does it?

Take the appropriate measures to protect yourself from the schemes you hear and read about. But never think you know it all. There is a reason that law enforcement's duty is not to stop crime, but to catch criminals after a crime has been committed. This is because confidence games are always changing and always progressing. Everyone else is behind. Even the playing field as best as you can. It can happen to anyone.

Remember, anyone can be a mark. Stay diligent and help those in need.

Take Everything

Just because confidence men are usually criminals by their very nature, does not mean they do not have skills and abilities that everyday people could employ, too. Lock picking sounds illegal, right? Maybe just shady at least. It is only illegal in all states if you do not have permission to pick the lock. If your good friend gets locked out of his home, office, or vehicle you could help him out if you only knew how to pick locks. This is just one skill many conmen have ingrained in their repertoire to facilitate their endeavors. Now, you do not have to know this particular skill but let us look at some things that should definitely be taken away from con men and used in your everyday life!

Critical Thinking and Problem Solving

Confidence men and con artists everywhere are presented with very unique problems and thus they must come up with ideas and strategies to combat these hindrances and obstacles. Taking their time, doing their research, and staying sharp is what keep con men on the forefront as problem solvers.

What they are faced with are very unique situations that probably have not been explored enough to have textbook solutions to solve them. If we can all just take a moment to think about what the real problem is, build up an idea, then muster the strength to carry it out we will be much better critical thinkers and problem solvers.

Do not think you cannot complete any task in front of you because of a minor disturbance. Conmen do an incredible amount of research, they stay current on topics in their particular field, and they regularly try to stay sharp by solving smaller problems more frequently. This type of routine gets them into the habit of thinking on their feet and being ready for any problem that arises. When something does happen, you will be ready.

Creativity

Stemming from point one, point two goes hand in hand. We all want to be more creative in every facet of our lives. Whether it is in art, fashion, writing, dating, or just what food to cook, creativity is the crux. Con men are some of the most creative people on Earth because they are in a constant state of motion. Guys like us either stay sharp or we get sloppy. Being creative assures con men that they are moving forward.

Not every idea is good, and you will make many mistakes in this area, but the sooner that is accepted the better off a person will be. Once an idea is formed and tested and does not work you will know to avoid that or to change it so eventually, it does work. Experience is key in this part of your life. Input is at the highest level of importance to being creative for a conman.

Take in everything, read books, watch people, and more importantly just remember that no knowledge is bad knowledge. Every piece of information has value under the right circumstances. Channel what you know to create new and exciting things in your own life.

Confidence

Where would a confidence man be without some confidence? The answer to that riddle, nowhere. Without confidence, no action can be truly successful. This only comes from being prepared, not only for what you expect to happen but also what you do not expect to happen. Everything you say and do should have purpose, not wasting your efforts to appease the visual cues of others. Make a statement as if everything you are saying and doing should be hung onto word for word and action for action. People will notice this and want to know what the secret is. Just because you do not know what the outcome of something will be, does not mean you cannot be confident. If you want to approach a person you think is attractive and ask them on a date you surely cannot know what will come from it. By being confident that no matter what happens you can handle it, you will give the notion that you have every idea as to what you are doing. This is a respectable trait and should be polished at every chance like a pair of crisp derby shoes before a soiree.

Dress to Impress

A long-time nod to the gentleman, con artists know when to wear the proper *costume* for their many roles. No role is more important than the everyday man they are. They never know when a great opportunity will arise to make some money or get something they really want. If you are dressed for the Ritz then guess what, you can get into any party that you want. Wear the clothes for the man (or woman) you want to be. The success will come later.

Talking my way into a New Year's Eve party at a very private, upscale venue would have been much harder had I not been dressed in proper attire. Had I been in daily garb? Slim chance I make it in without being accosted. Dress with all that confidence you got from reading point three.

Dealing with Pressure

No person on this planet goes without having to deal with at least a little bit of pressure in their life. Some of us go each day with many pressures. Dealing with these situations is an element all con artists are well adept with. In the life of a con man you never know when something might go terribly wrong and having that pressure on your shoulders to consistently deliver is enough to break many men.

This is different from problem-solving as there is an added stress from the small percentage of things that cannot be accounted for and for the perilous situations professional grifters find themselves in.

Remember to take your time and think about what you want to do and how much time you have to do it is a daily regimen practice never to be ignored.

As always, trust is given to the readers to make good decisions and do no harm to those around you.

Silver Tongued Devil

The term *silver tongue* has always fascinated me. Now that I have a platform to share my thoughts and ideas, I want to share with the reader just what this means and why it is a great tool for scammers and confidence men.

Having a silver tongue has become synonymous with being a confidence man.

It is just a way of saying that a particular person uses their words and speech to get what they want. They do not rely on a physical skill or a trade every time to get what they desire.

Being able to talk themselves in or out of any situation is their greatest asset. Silver is valuable and so is their tongue.

Learning to put syllables together in a way that elicits a certain response from another human and be in control of it is possibly one of the greatest abilities any mortal could hope to possess.

Influence is something all powerful people strive for. Some do it with money, or threats, or fear.

The con man relies strictly on words to get the results he wants. He is not above saying what has to be said, or not said.

If you want to keep up with the world we live in, then you too will have to learn to use your words. Not necessarily in a deceptive manner, but in such a way to convey what you want, what you need, and what you expect.

Once you can determine what it is you desire, and you know what you want to say to get to the end result then you simply speak with confidence and add that to actions that also reflect confidence.

Eloquence, finesse, poise, grace, confidence; these are all words that should be in the back of your mind when you are speaking. They are always at the forefront of a con man's mind when he speaks. This is why people do what he wants and do not question him.

We can learn something from everyone. Con men are no exception. If we take their tactics and techniques and add them to our lives, then we will begin to grow beyond many of the traditional swindles and deceptions at play in this world.

I am only giving one example of how we can grow ourselves and push to be better all around. Do not stop searching for ways to better yourself and your life.

Get Away With It

This is the part that matters most and least to a criminal. He (or she) wants to get away with it quite badly, but yet, they seldom go through the trouble of planning out their end game.

I believe that someone cannot *get away with it* if even a single person knows what they have done.

For instance, fleeing the country. Well you might have gotten away from the scene of the crime, but you have not escaped suspicion. If all the evidence says you did it. Then you have not gotten away with it. You just have not been caught yet.

To truly get away with something is to do it and no one even suspects you.

I make a point to talk about this because I want the reader to be hopeful that if someone defrauds them, scams them, or cons them, they know the scammer will not be able to get away with it. Strictly based on my theory of suspicion killing any chance of truly getting away with it.

Knowing someone did something to you and getting justice for what they did are two different things, though. I understand that to the fullest. But be hopeful and trust in your own knowledge that you gain from this book and beyond, that the scammer will find his penance.

Getting away with it is just the scammer fooling himself. He is fooling himself if he thinks he can get away with his crimes. There may be momentary reprieves where there is not a pursuit for him, but that pursuit will, at some point, resume. Getting away with it is almost the biggest scam of them all. He is almost tricking himself into a belief that he is safe and that he can bask in his success. This is but a temporary break from reality.

Social Engineering

In the world of deception some players would like to shield themselves from negative spotlights, from negative terms that could cast a very ugly shadow onto them. They wish to hide their deceptive nature and their thoughts of swindling and finessing and fleecing marks. One method for dissolving these terms is by conjuring up new ones. Brand new terms that may misrepresent their true meaning. Essentially, *doublespeak* with tones of actuality.

Social engineering is used in the field of security of information and networks to describe actions taken to get a person to divulge information that could be used to infiltrate a brick and mortar facility or a network or both.

By identifying deception, in this realm, as *social engineering* the bad vibes of deception are cast off and watered down. At its core is social engineering not lying, deceiving, and manipulating a person or people? Why not call a con a con? By avoiding the terms regularly accepted, individuals in this field can skirt the negative connotations of *lying, cheating, stealing, conning,* and *manipulating.* This may be an ongoing disservice to what they are attempting to convey to their clients and their audience. Avoiding these terms may also send the wrong message about the morality and ethics of manipulation by design. The ideas of fundamentals found in literature on social engineering is, for the most part, sound. It deals with techniques used by confidence men around the globe.

As it relates to network security the terms change. *Social engineering* becomes the umbrella term, a seemingly pointless shift. Perhaps this shift is made to make a point that the subject is referring solely to network security and the tactics used to circumvent them through manipulation of people and patterns within.

When unnecessary distinctions are made that allow non-deceptive peoples to rebrand terms in order to fit their own morals and ethics it betrays the core of the terms. By creating this *genre* of work in the field of deception it opens a door to allow all terms to be redefined and to allow terms to no longer matter. It sounds as if someone wants to do things they shouldn't be doing but want it to sound nice and pleasant, so they can be given a pass from society. *Oh, it's not manipulation. It's not trickery and deception, it's just social engineering.*

Perhaps those who wish to be deceptive and wish to deceive others for whatever altruistic reason they conjured up just do not want people to think they are a bad person. They would like to be accepted as a good person who just has to dip their toe into the black lagoon of deception in order to keep the peace and thwart evil doers. This type of work can be done without rebranding terms in order to make themselves feel better about the what they are doing. Users of the term *social engineering* are hiding behind a form of doublespeak and disguising its nature.

There are instances where we have to call a spade a spade. This is one such instance. For now, the term social engineering can coexist with the vocabulary of confidence games and the like, but if it expands any further it will only further cause confusion that will aid confidence men. Potential marks will misunderstand deception more than they already do.

Gobbledygook

Speaking of terms that make less than zero sense. What on earth is a *scam artist?* We know what a *con artist* is, but what is a scam artist? Maybe this a scammer who paints in his spare time between cold calling marks about their expired car warranty and sending phishing emails swearing to be able to increase the size of your...wallet. Scams are everywhere, all the time. Also, art is everywhere, too, I guess. I digress.

Scammers are scammers, there is not much more to say on this. Scam artist sounds like a high brow term a bureaucrat invented accidentally when preparing his ninety second PowerPoint presentation for a regular Monday meeting. Oh, scammer, confidence man, con artist, swindler, it is really all the same, right? *The sound of words being mashed incessantly together lingers.*

Scammers are not artists, everything they do requires almost no skill and their

103

scams are tossed like a fishing net in a lagoon where the water has just evaporated suddenly, leaving all of the fish stranded and ready to be netted. Calling scammers *scam artists* or some other term that does not relate adds more confusion, and frankly, shows that the person speaking on the subject has no in-depth knowledge or experience to draw from when these discussions arise.

Gobbledygook[14] is a form of *doublespeak*, nonsensical overly technical sounding terms that are jumbled and create a gibberish term that is difficult to decipher for readers or listeners.

How could a reader ever expect to gain usable knowledge on confidence games if every media outlet, piece of writing, article or book cannot even call scammers by their name? By now it should be evident that there

---

[14] Vocabulary.com defines *gobbledygook* as such: incomprehensible or pompous jargon of specialists.

are many terms that simply cannot be switched out arbitrarily in order to sound cool or to sound as though the creator of the content is some deception expert. Terminology has importance because it allows corrections to be made and put in place to thwart scams, frauds, and confidence games.

Final Words

There was no moment during the writing of this collection of essays that was not spent wondering what ideas and opinions should be kept quiet until a later date. All that has been revealed from my mind on these pages was for the purpose of encouraging everyone to *think* and change their ways of thinking or explore new ways of thinking as it pertains to confidence games. If we become too rigid and do not adapt to the deceptions circling us regularly we will die with the times. Sharks are only dangerous to you if you are in the water, we act according to their environment. We share an environment with confidence men and we have to learn that they can break us, and we can only rely on ourselves on a day to day basis for protection. Working in the field of deceptions, confidence games, scams and swindles presents incredibly unique obstacles as this field is not understood by the everyman, even on the surface level. What would be considered *basic* knowledge is still more than the public could muster.

Bringing awareness to the field of deception in a meaningful way gives the public a chance to fight back and understand growing problems that they could face each day. For the most part, this book could be considered a personal commentary on confidence games and confidence men. By its own virtue confidence games are secretive and not well studied. Embezzlement, white collar crime as a whole, and financial fraud as groups are decently well covered, but there is a slice of the pie that does not get the full doppler coverage, confidence games and scams. It is painfully apparent because if it was covered correctly there would not be nearly as many mistakes published in articles and in media with such high frequency.

When a product hits the open market that could be dangerous to someone's health if used improperly or used without the utmost care, there are warnings to accompany said products. The creator of the acetylene torches warns of why improper use could result in injury or serious bodily harm. Yet, these items are still available for purchase. This is because consumers accept the warnings and heed them when operating the torch. They have put in the work, so we do not have to. The same could be said for this book, its predecessors and its successors. The work has been put in, the fat cut off, and the words sharpened to better help the reader.

Acknowledgements:

Dylan Sherman –

an almost violently positive person. A man whose ideas and passion have shaped my own. A friend and brother.

Oliver Francis –

Oli is an artist in his own right. Creating music that gave my long nights a bit more zest. A person who cares about his craft as much as anyone can.

Daniel Madison –

perhaps the reasons I decided I could record my thoughts on paper for the public. His work has always been and will always be a driving force for me. He has set the bar so high that I will always work to match up and one day, surpass.

Neema Atri –

the most gifted writer to never get the full volume of appreciation he deserves. He is an actor, a magician, a genius, and a friend. Advice and wise words have been shared

more than a time or two. I will owe you for
an eternity for your guidance.

Brian Graham –

for years he encouraged me. His well of
positive words never dries. His cup runneth
over in terms of ideas and pure creativity.
One day he will be creating life changing
projects for everyone to stand in awe of.

Made in United States
Cleveland, OH
18 December 2024

12045055R00061